D1135210

This b...

Why Manners Matter

At Home

HIGHLAND LIBRARIES

WITHDRAWN

Jillian Powell

W

FRANKLIN WATTS
LONDON • SYDNEY

First published in 2005 by
Franklin Watts
96 Leonard Street
London
EC2A 4XD

Franklin Watts Australia
45-51 Huntley Street
Alexandria, NSW 2015

© Franklin Watts 2005

Editor: Rachel Tonkin
Series design: Mo Choy
Art director: Jonathan Hair
Photography: Chris Fairclough
PSHE Consultant: Wendy Anthony

With thanks to our models: Jack Young, Eve Steere,
Molly Steere and Daisy Steere

A CIP catalogue record for this book is
available from the British Library

Dewey classification 395.5

ISBN: 0 7496 6050 3

Printed in China

THE HIGHLAND COUNCIL
SCHOOLS LIBRARY
RESOURCE SERVICE

Contents

Thinking of others

Your home is where you live. You have to share it with other people.

It's important to think about other people's feelings at home. It will make your home a happy place for everyone.

? Who shares your home with you?

Sharing things

You have to share things at home. It can be fun if you are fair and make sure everyone gets a turn.

? What do you
have to share at home?

Sharing a room can be hard.
It's nicer if you try to stay
friends and keep things tidy.

Helping out

There are lots of ways you can help at home. You can help to lay the table or clear it after a meal.

What jobs do you
help with at home?

You can help by sharing jobs
like the washing up.

Caring for things

You should look after things in your home. Beds are for sleeping in, not to jump on.

Take care to turn off lights when you are not using them. This way, you can look after your home and save electricity, too.

Listening and talking

Sometimes you have to be patient when you want to speak to someone. You should wait quietly if they are busy.

If people are talking,
you can join in, too,
but only when they've
finished speaking.

?
Why
is it rude
to interrupt
someone?

13

Table manners

At the dinner table, you should wait until everyone has their plate before you start to eat.

? What do you do if you can't reach something you want on the table?

When you ask for something at the table, remember to say please and thank you.

Eating

When you are eating, it is important to use a knife and fork properly.

Why should
you wash your hands
before you eat?

Don't stuff too much food into
your mouth or eat with your
mouth open. Other people don't
want to see what you are chewing.

17

Saying sorry

You should remember to say sorry when you break or spill something at home.

If you have been nasty to someone, always say sorry. Think how you feel when someone is nasty to you.

Safety at home

If you drop something on the floor, it is important to clear it up before it causes an accident.

? What might happen if the floor is messy?

When you have finished playing with toys, always put them away safely. If you don't, they may cause an accident.

Think about . . .

When you are sharing a meal with your family and friends, there are lots of things you should think about . . .

? What do you say when someone gives you some food or a drink?

? How do you ask for someone to pass something to you?

? What should you say when you want to get down from the table?

? What should you do if you drop or spill something?

Think about why manners matter
when you are playing at home with
your family or with your friends . . .

? What should
you say if you upset
someone?

? Why should
you share your toys?

? What should
you do when you
have finished playing
with toys or games?

? What should
you do if you break
or spoil something at
home?

Index